Illinois State Historical

APRIL 1910

LINCOLN'S DEFENSE OF DUFF ARMSTRONG
THE STORY OF THE TRIAL AND
THE CELEBRATED ALMANAC

By
J. N. GRIDLEY
Virginia, Illinois

Re-Print from the Journal of the Society of April 1910

LINCOLN'S DEFENSE OF DUFF ARMSTRONG.
The Story of the Trial and Celebrated Almanac.

About forty years ago, the writer, a young man, and a comparative stranger in Beardstown, Illinois, heard a conversation in that city between two persons, not known to him. One of them, whom I will designate as Brown, was telling the other of the trial of Duff Armstrong in Beardstown in the spring of 1858. Brown said that he heard the trial; that a witness for the People testified that the prisoner assaulted the deceased at 10 o'clock at night; that the moon was directly overhead, and it was as light as day; that he stood near by, and saw Armstrong strike the deceased several terrible blows with a slung shot. Brown said the State's Attorney then rested his case, and the court adjourned for the day. That night Lincoln went to a drug store at the corner of the square on State street and procured a number of almanacs, which he took to his room, and with them "manufactured" an almanac which showed there was no moon on the night of the assault; this "doctored" almanac was introduced to the jury and resulted in the acquittal of the prisoner. Brown said that Lincoln was a very able and shrewd lawyer, thus to be able to deceive the court and jury and to succeed in clearing his client. A few years previous to this conversation I had attended political meetings, held in Michigan, during the campaign of 1860, and heard the republican candidate spoken of as "Honest Old Abe," and thought if the management of this Armstrong case was a specimen of his honesty, that he did not deserve the appellation.

In Barrett's "Life of Lincoln," in referring to this trial, the author, after describing the testimony of the prosecuting witness as to the position of the moon says:

"At this point Mr. Lincoln produced an almanac which showed that at the time referred to by the witness there was no moon at all, and showed it to the jury."

Herndon, in his "Life of Lincoln," in which he gives an account of this trial, says:

"Lincoln floored the principal prosecuting witness, who had testified positively to seeing the fatal blow struck in the moonlight, by showing from an almanac that the moon had set."

In February 1909, the ladies of Beardstown, Illinois, held a public meeting in commemoration of the birth of Abraham Lincoln; they had assigned to different members of their club subjects upon which to prepare papers to be read upon the anniversary occasion. To Mrs. Dr. Schweer was assigned the task of writing up the "Armstrong Trial." This lady visited Mr. A. P. Armstrong, of Ashland, a town thirty miles distant from Beardstown—this gentleman was a brother to Duff Armstrong. A. P. Armstrong was born in 1840, and was 17 years of age when his brother was tried. Mrs. Schweer relied upon the statements of this brother which she used in the preparation of her very well written paper, from which I make the following quotation:

"A fellow by the name of Allen, from Petersburg, was the chief witness for the State, and whether he was the one who really killed this Metzker, or (as some thought, he had fallen from his horse in a drunken stupor and died from the injuries received), we do not know. However, Allen was sworn in as chief witness for the State.

"The case was finally brought up for trial. The Armstrongs had taken this Allen to Virginia and had him put away in the old Virginia house, so that he could not testify, but Lincoln insisted on his being brought into the court room.

"Collier, of Petersburg, was State's Attorney. He gave his testimony, and showed, what appeared to the audience, a strong proof of murder. Lincoln cross-examined very little, only looking up and ascertaining a few dates and places. His own witnesses were to show comparatively good moral character for the prisoner previous to the time of the murder. Collier, feeling sure of his case, made but a short and formal argument. Then Lincoln followed for the defense. He began calmly, slowly and carefully. He struck at the very heart of the State's evidence, that of the chief witness, Allen. He followed up first one discrepancy, then another, and then another; finally he came to that part of the testimony of the chief witness where he had sworn positively by the light of the moon he had seen the prisoner deliver the fatal blow with a sling-shot. Then he asked a cousin of Armstrong, Jake Jones by name, to go out and get him an almanac at the nearest store.

"Taking this almanac Lincoln showed that on the night sworn to and the hour sworn to, the moon had not risen, proving that the whole of this testimony was a perjury."

The reader of this part of the account would naturally wonder why Allen would commit perjury in order to send Duff Armstrong to the gallows, when he had agreed to stay away at the instance of Armstrong's friends. A reluctant witness, who is brought into the witness box by an attachment, is not likely to swear falsely to aid the cause of the party that dragged him into court.

Having read these various accounts, and having heard from numerous persons of the fraudulent almanac, and being absolutely unable to believe that Abraham Lincoln would be guilty of such outrageous conduct, I concluded to look into the matter, late as it was.

I first directed a letter to the Professor of Astronomy of the University of Illinois, inquiring the position of the moon in this latitude and longitude on the night of

August 29th, 1857, when the assault was committed. In reply he wrote me as follows:

"URBANA, ILL., March 2, 1909.

MR. J. N. GRIDLEY,
    Virginia, Illinois;

DEAR SIR:

Answering yours of Febr. 24, the moon was at first quarter Aug. 27, 1857, at 9 A. M. On the night of August 29 the moon was two days and a half past first quarter, and crossed the meridian at 7:44 P. M. local time. The time of moonset, was within 15 minutes of midnight, but to give this closer, I would have to know the exact locality for which to compute.

Trusting that this information is what you want, I am,
            Very truly yours,
                    JOEL STEBBINS,
                        Director Observatory."

To a second letter I received the following reply:

"URBANA, ILL., March 29, 1909.

MR. J. N. GRIDLEY,
    Virginia, Illinois;

DEAR SIR:

I have been rather busy of late and have neglected answering your last letter.

I computed the time of moonset for Longitude 90 degrees west of Greenwich, and Latitude 40 degrees.

For August 29, 1857, I find the moonset at 12 h 05 m., i. e. five minutes after midnight of August 29.

You understand this refers to the disappearance of the moon's upper edge below the true horizon.

I am sorry that I cannot inform you about the period called the 'dark of the moon.' It may have an exact meaning but I cannot find the term used in any of the text-books, or in any standard work. I am under the impression that the period extends from last quarter until new moon, but that is only a guess. In 1857 there was new moon on August 19, 10 A. M.; first quarter

John T. Brady, the sole survivor of the jury that tried
Duff Armstrong at Beardstown, Ill., May 7, 1858.

you have, full moon on Sept. 3d, 11 P. M. and last quarter on Sept. 10, 5 P. M.

Hoping that this is suitable for your purpose, I am,
Very truly yours,
JOEL STEBBINS,
Director Observatory."

The reader can now see that if an almanac was introduced at the Armstrong trial that showed there was no moon to be seen at 10 P. M., the hour all the witnesses agreed the assault took place, that the Court and the jury were deceived.

Having proceeded thus far, I examined the record to learn whether any of the jurors were living, who might be able to remember the details of the trial. I found the names of the jurors were as follows: Horace Hill, Milton Logan, Nelson Graves, Charles D. Marcy, John T. Brady, Thornton M. Cole, George F. Sielschott, Samuel W. Neely, Matthew Armstrong, Benjamin Eyre, John M. Johnson, and Augustus Hoyer.

I knew two of these jurors, Milton Logan and John T. Brady, both of whom were then living, and to them I addressed letters of inquiry. I received no answer from Mr. Logan, and learned that his memory had wholly failed him;; he died in Feb. 1910 at his home in Boone, Iowa, at the advanced age of 90 years.

I became acquainted with Mr. John T. Brady in 1864, when he was visiting his friends in this county on a furlough from his regiment in the Union Army. He was then a citizen of Kansas; I have met him frequently since that date, and last summer had the pleasure of visiting him and his family at their home in Pomona, California. He is a retired capitalist, in the enjoyment of excellent physical health, and his mental powers unimpaired. He is a man of much more than ordinary intelligence, and he has written me at length, of his recollections of the Armstrong trial, and I have every confidence in the reliability of his information. I have carefully examined the record of the trial, have written to Judge Lyman Lacey, of Havana, Ill., who, with his former partner, William Walker, also represented Duff Armstrong in this trial; I also have interviewed Mr. A. P. Armstrong, the brother before mentioned, and believe that I have learned the truth in the matter of this trial.

There is nothing remarkable in the history of this trial; but in order to state the facts, and to correct the wrong impressions that have been made by the various accounts of the trial, this paper has been prepared.

In August 1857, a religious camp-meeting was held in Mason county, Illinois, at a grove about six miles northeast of the junction of Salt Creek with Sangamon River, and about seven miles southwest of Mason City. Camp meetings were common in those days, as country churches were then few and far between. They usually continued for ten days or two weeks; the tents of canvass, or rough sheds of lumber were built on the circumference of a circle; stands four feet square and four feet high were erected within the circle, constructed of posts and covered with earth, upon which bright fires were kept burning through the night, attended by watchers, who guarded the sleepers from the attacks of outlaws, who infested this country, who delighted to annoy quiet people whenever they had the slightest opportunity. These tough characters amused themselves by running horses, drinking whiskey, and fighting. This camp meeting was due to close on Sunday, August 30, 1857. On the afternoon of Saturday, August 29th quite a number of men had gathered about the huckster's wagons that were encamped a short distance (perhaps a quarter of a mile) south of the tents. Among these men was Duff Armstrong, then a young man of 24 years, who owned a race horse and who was very fond of running it. He was not a vicious man, was kind hearted, and friendly, but fond of whiskey, as most young men of those days in that section were. He had been indulging in drinking on that Saturday afternoon, and had also been engaged in horse racing. He had become intoxicated, and early in the evening was lying upon a bench or table sleeping off his drunkenness. About seven or eight o'clock P. M. James P. Metzker, a farmer, who lived near Petersburg in Menard county, a few miles southeast of the Salt Creek camp ground, arrived on the scene. Metzker is said to have been quarrelsome when in liquor, and, it is said, came there in an intoxicated condition, riding a horse. Seeing Duff Armstrong lying on the bench asleep, he seized him by the leg, and dragged him to the ground; Armstrong being partially drunk, and half asleep and thoroughly angered, attacked Metzker, and a fight ensued. The character of this attack was discussed at the trial, and will be commented upon later. A. P. Armstrong says he was present and witnessed the affair, says that after the fight, Metzker and his brother Duff shook hands and drank together, and soon after J. H. Norris and Metzker had a fight. Metzker mounted his horse and started homeward at a late hour, and, it is said, fell from his horse one or more times, being greatly under the influence of liquor. The third day after this trouble Metzker died and Norris and Armstrong were arrested for murder, and on account of the great excitement of the people over the affair, and because the Mason county jail at Havana, Ill., was rather insecure, the prisoners were taken across the Illinois river into the adjoining county of Fulton, and incarcerated in the jail at Lewiston.

At the October term, 1857, of the Mason County Circuit, both Norris and Armstrong were jointly indicted for the murder of Metzker. The indictment was as follows:

State of Illinois,
Mason County.

> Of the October Term of the Mason County Circuit Court in the year of Our Lord one thousand eight hundred and fifty-seven.

The Grand Jurors chosen selected and sworn in and for the County of Mason aforesaid in the name and by the authority of the People of the State of Illinois upon their oaths present that James H. Norris and William Armstrong late of the County of Mason and State of Illinois not having the fear of God before their eyes, but being moved and seduced by the instigation of the Devil, on the twenty-ninth day of August in the year of Our Lord one thousand eight hundred and fifty-seven with force and arms at and within the County of Mason and State of Illinois, in and upon one James Preston Metzker in the peace of the said People of the said State of Illinois then and there being, unlawfully, feloniously, willfully, and of their malice aforethought did make an assault. And the said James H. Norris with a certain piece of wood about three feet long which he the said James H. Norris in his right hand then and there held the said James Preston Metzker in and upon the back part of the head of him the said James Preston Metzker then and there unlawfully, feloniously, willfully, and of his malice aforethought, did strike, giving to the said James Preston Metzker then and there with the stick of wood aforesaid in and upon the said back part of the head of him the said James Preston Metzker, one mortal bruise and the said William Armstrong with a certain hard metallic substance called a slung-shot which he the said William Armstrong in his right hand then and there had and held, the said James Preston Metzker, in and upon the right eye of him the said James Preston Metzker then and there unlawfully, feloniously, willfully and of his malice aforethought did strike, giving to the said James Preston Metzker then and there with a slung-shot aforesaid in and upon the said right eye of him the said James Preston Metzker one other mortal bruise, of which said mortal bruises the said James Preston Metzker from the said 29th. day of August in the year aforesaid until the 1st day of September in the year aforesaid at the County of Mason and State of Illinois aforesaid did languish, and languishing did live on which said first day of September in the year aforesaid the said James Preston Metzker in the County and State aforesaid of the said mortal bruises died; and so the jurors aforesaid upon their oaths aforesaid do say that the said James H. Norris and William Armstrong the said James Preston Metzker in manner and form aforesaid unlawfully, feloniously, and of their malice aforethought did kill and murder contrary to the form of the statute in such cases made and provided and against the Peace and dignity of the same People of the State of Illinois.

And the Grand Jurors aforesaid in the name and by the authority aforesaid upon their oaths aforesaid do further present James H. Norris and William Armstrong late of the County of Mason and State of Illinois not having the fear of God before their eyes but being moved and seduced by the instigation of the Devil, on the twenty-ninth day of August in the year of Our Lord one thousand eight hundred and fifty-seven with force and arms at and within the County of Mason and State of Illinois in and upon one James Preston Metzker in the Peace of the said People of the said State of Illinois then and there being unlawfully feloniously, and willfully and of their malice aforethought did make an assault; and that the said James H. Norris and William Armstrong with a certain hard metallic substance commonly called a slung-shot which they the said James H. Norris and William Armstrong in both their right hands then and there had and held, the said James Preston Metzker in and upon the right eye of him the said James Preston Metzker then and there unlawfully, feloniously, willfully and of their malice aforethought did strike, beat and bruise, giving to the said James Preston Metzker then and there with the slung-shot aforesaid by striking, beating and bruising the said James Preston Metzker in and upon the right eye of him the said James Preston Metzker one other mortal bruise of which said mortal bruise the said James Preston Metzker from the said twenty-ninth day of August in the year of Our Lord one thousand eight hundred and fifty-seven aforesaid until the first day of September in the year aforesaid at the County of Mason and State of Illinois aforesaid did languish, and languishing did live on which first day of September in the year aforesaid the said James Preston Metzker in the county and State aforesaid of the said mortal bruise died. And so the jurors aforesaid upon their oaths aforesaid do say that the said James H. Norris and William Armstrong the said James Preston Metzker in manner and form aforesaid unlawfully, feloniously, willfully and of their malice aforethought did kill and murder contrary to the form of the statute in such cases made and provided and against the Peace and Dignity of the same People of the State of Illinois.

And the Grand Jurors aforesaid upon their oaths aforesaid in the name and by the authority of the People aforesaid do further present James H. Norris and William Armstrong late of the County of Mason and State of Illinois on the twenty-ninth day of August in the year of Our Lord one thousand eight hundred and fifty-seven not having the fear of God before their eyes, but being moved and seduced by the instigation of the Devil with force and arms at and within the County of Mason and State of Illinois in and upon the said James Preston Metzker in the Peace of the People of the said State of Illinois then and there being, unlawfully, feloniously, willfully and of their malice aforethought did make an assault; and that the said James H Norris and William Armstrong with a certain stick of wood three feet long and of the diameter of two inches which they the said James H Norris and William Armstrong in their right hands then and there had and held the said James Preston Metzker in and upon the back side of the head of him the said James Preston Metzker then and there feloniously, willfully, unlawfully, and of their malice aforethought did strike, beat and bruise, giving to the said James Preston Metzker then and there with a stick of wood aforesaid in and upon the said back side of the head of him the said James Preston Metzker one other mortal bruise of which said mortal bruise the said James Preston Metzker on the said twenty-ninth day of August in the year aforesaid until the first day of September in the year aforesaid at the County and State aforesaid did languish and languishing did live on which said first day of September in the year aforesaid at the County and State aforesaid of the said mortal bruise died; and so the Jurors aforesaid upon their oaths aforesaid do say that the said James H. Norris and William Armstrong the said James Preston Metzker in manner and form aforesaid, unlawfully feloniously, willfully, and of their malice aforethought did kill and murder; contrary to the form of the statute in such cases made and provided and against the Peace and Dignity of the same People of the State of Illinois.

HUGH FULLERTON,
States Attorney.

Filed November 5th 1857.

Witnesses: Grigsby Z. Metzker, Charles Allen, James P. Walker, William M. Hall, Joseph A. Douglas, William Douglas, B. F. Stephenson, Hamilton Rogers, William Killion, Joseph Speltz and William Haines.

Not bailable: James Harriott.

The defendant Norris, had, before that time, killed a man named Thornsbury, and had been indicted for his murder, but was cleared on a plea of self defense; perhaps, on account of this record, he labored under a disadvantage; he stated to the court, that he was unable to employ counsel, and the judge (James Harriott) appointed William Walker, who was the senior partner of Lyman Lacey, who was then a young man of some 26 years, to defend Norris. In the meantime, Dilworth and Campbell, attorneys of the Mason County bar, had applied for a change of venue from Mason County, Armstrong having made affidavit that the people of that County were so prejudiced against him, that he could not have a fair trial. Judge Harriott ordered the venue, as to Armstrong, changed to Cass County, which is in the same Circuit and adjoined Mason County on the south. Walker and Dilworth and Campbell defended Norris, in Mason County, and Hugh Fullerton, the State's Attorney of the Circuit prosecuted him. The jury found Norris guilty, and he was sentenced to the Penitentiary for the term of eight years.

While Duff Armstrong was lying in the Fulton county jail, his father Jack Armstrong died; on his death bed he advised his wife, Hannah Armstrong, to save Duff if she could, if she had to give up her little farm of forty acres. She employed Walker and Lacey to look after Duff's defense at Havana.

Upon the adjournment of the Mason County Circuit Court, the Mason County sheriff, started to the state penitentiary, then at Alton, Illinois; by steam boat down the Illinois river from Havana to Alton; as Beardstown was on the route, the sheriff handcuffed Norris and Armstrong together and began the journey. While on the way, Norris urged Armstrong to walk about the boat with him, but Armstrong complained of weariness, and kept his seat. He afterwards explained to his friends that he feared Norris might attempt to escape, and drag him overboard. Arriving at Beardstown, the two men were separated, and Duff Armstrong was locked up in the Cass county jail, in that city, and Norris taken down to Alton.

In the meantime Mrs. Hannah Armstrong was advised to secure the services of her old friend Abraham Lincoln.

Rev. J. T. Hobson, of Lake City, Iowa, in 1909 published an interesting little book entitled, "Footprints of

Abraham Lincoln." This work was published by The Otterbein Press of Dayton, Ohio. This author states that Mr. Lincoln addressed a letter to Mrs. Armstrong as follows:

Springfield, Ohio, [?] September 18, ——
"Dear Mrs. Armstrong:—I have just heard of your deep affliction, and the arrest of your son for murder. I can hardly believe that he can be guilty of the crime alleged against him. It does not seem possible. I am anxious that he should have a fair trial, at any rate; and gratitude for your long continued kindness to me in adverse circumstances prompts me to offer my humble services gratuitously in his behalf. It will afford me an opportunity to requite, in a small degree, the favors I received at your hand, and that of your lamented husband, when your roof afforded me grateful shelter without money and without price.
Yours truly,
Abraham Lincoln."

In August, 1831, Abraham Lincoln, then a youth of 22 years, made his appearance in New Salem, Menard county, Illinois, a small settlement on the Sangamon river, a few miles above Petersburg, Illinois. He was employed as a clerk by a man named Offut, who was the proprietor of a store. Offut very soon became a warm friend of his young clerk. He boasted that Lincoln could outrun, whip, or throw down any man in Sangamon county. (Menard was then a part of Sangamon.) A quotation from "Herndon's Life of Lincoln reads thus:

"In the neighborhood of the village (of New Salem), or rather a few miles to the southwest, lay a strip of timber called Clary's Grove. The boys who lived there were a terror to the entire region—seemingly a necessary product of frontier civilization. They were friendly and good natured; they could trench a pond, dig a bog, build a house; they could pray and fight, make a village or create a state. They would do almost anything for sport or fun, love or necessity. Though rude and rough, though life's forces ran over the edge of the bowl, foaming and sparkling in pure deviltry's sake, yet place before them a poor man who needed their aid, a lame or sick man, a defenseless woman, a widow, they melted into sympathy and charity at once. They gave all they had, and willingly toiled or played cards for more. Though there never was under the sun a more generous parcel of rowdies, a stranger's introduction was likely to be the most unpleasant part of his acquaintance with them. They conceded leadership to one Jack Armstrong, a hardy, strong, and well-developed specimen of physical manhood, and under him they were in the habit of "cleaning out" New Salem whenever his order went forth to do so. Offut and "Bill" Clary—the latter skeptical of Lincoln's strength and agility—ended a heated discussion in the store one day over the new clerk's ability to meet the tactics of Clary's Grove, by a bet of ten dollars that Jack Armstrong was, in the language of the day, "a better man than Lincoln." The new clerk strongly opposed this sort of an introduction, but after much entreaty from Offut, at last consented to make his bow to the social lions of the town in this unusual way. He was now six feet four inches high, and weighed, as his friend and confidant, William Green, tells us with impressive precision, "two hundred and fourteen pounds." The great contest was to be a friendly one and fairly conducted. All New Salem adjourned to the scene of the wrestle. Money, whiskey, knives and all manner of property were staked on the result. It is unnecessary to go into the details of the encounter. Every one knows how it ended; how at last the tall and angular railsplitter, enraged at the suspicion of foul tactics, and profiting by his height and the length of his arms, fairly lifted the great bully by the throat and shook him like a rag; how by this act he established himself solidly in the esteem of all New Salem, and secured the respectful admiration of the very man whom he had so thoroughly vanquished. From this time forward Jack Armstrong, his wife Hannah, and all the other Armstrongs became his warm and trusted friends. None stood readier than they to rally to his support, none more willing to lend a helping hand. Lincoln appreciated their friendship and support, and in after years proved his gratitude by saving one member of the family from the gallows.''

Shortly after the above encounter, Lincoln became a member of the Armstrong family. The family then lived three and a half miles north of Petersburg, Menard county, two or three miles from the Sangamon river, near Concord church. Here the future president made rails, studied surveying, and helped the farmers of the neighborhood with their work. Mrs. Armstrong would often tell of having "foxed" Lincoln's trousers with deer skin, so they would better sustain the rough usage to which they were subjected in his surveying trips, through tall prairie grass, timber and brush, which he travelled through in establishing the lines of the lands of the early settlers.

Mrs. Armstrong drove all the way to Springfield to consult Mr. Lincoln, hoping he might be able to secure the release of her son before his trial.

Mr. Lincoln attended the November Term of the Cass Circuit court in order to get his client admitted to bail. The result of this effort is shown by the following transcript of the record of the court:

November 19, 1857. The People of the State of Illinois vs. William Armstrong; Venue from Mason County.

And now on this day come the People of the State of Illinois, by their attorney, Hugh Fullerton, Esquire, and the prisoner William Armstrong, who is brought here to the Bar in proper person. A motion is made by the prisoner, to admit him to Bail. Whereupon a motion was made on the part of the People for a continuance until the next Term of this Court, which, after due deliberation by the Court, was granted, and the motion to admit to Bail, was overruled.

Mr. Lincoln then told Duff that he must remain in jail until the next spring, and then he would come down and get him out. Mrs. Armstrong was present at this time. An old school teacher, who was confined in the same jail for larceny, proposed to Duff's mother, that if she would buy him a pair of spectacles and some books, he would teach her son to read during the long hours that were to come, before the advent of spring; the mother gladly did this, and Duff emerged from the jail the following May, very thin and pale, but his education had been much improved.

The May term of the Circuit Court of Cass county convened on Monday the 3d instant; Mr. Lincoln arrived on Thursday the 6th, and found that the most important witness for the People, Charles Allen, had not arrived, and that an attachment had been issued for him. He inquired of the friends of Armstrong what they knew of Allen, and was told that Allen had agreed with them to remain at the hotel at Virginia, 13 miles away, provided his expenses were paid, and in case they wanted him present, he would come if they would come after him. Mr. Lincoln soon explained to them that if Allen did not appear, he having been summoned to come, the case would be continued, and Duff would remain in jail for six months to come. Two cousins of Duff hitched up the team to their wagon and drove off to Virginia and brought Allen into Beardstown that night, and on Friday the 7th instant, the trial began. The case was prosecuted by Hugh Fullerton, the State's Attorney, assisted by an attorney named Collier, from Petersburg, who had been employed by a brother of Metzker, the deceased. Mr. Lincoln was assisted by William Walker, the senior member of the firm of Walker & Lacey, of Havana, Illinois.

I will allow Mr. Brady, the only juror now living, who tried this case, to describe the trial in his own way:

"The prosecuting witness, Allen, testified in the trial that the reason he could see a slung-shot that Armstrong had in his hand, with which he struck Metzker, was that the moon was shining very bright, about where the sun would be, at one o'clock in the afternoon. Mr. Lincoln was very particular to have him repeat himself a dozen or more times during the trial about where the moon was located, and my recollection is now, that the almanac was not introduced until Mr. Lincoln came to that part of Allen's testimony telling the Court where the moon was located. Mr. Lincoln was very careful not to cross Mr. Allen in anything, and when Allen lacked words to express himself, Lincoln loaned them to him. Allen was the only witness for the State, and there were eight or ten witnesses for the defense, and they all swore that Armstrong struck Metzker with his fist, and I am satisfied that the jury thought Allen was telling the truth. I know that he impressed me that way, but his evidence with reference to the moon was so far from the facts that it destroyed his evidence with the jury. The almanac that was produced was examined closely by the Court, and the attorneys for the State, and the almanac showed that the moon at that time was going out of sight; setting; and the almanac was allowed to be used as evidence by Judge Harriott.

There has never been a question in my mind about the genuineness of the almanac, that it was an up to date almanac; this I am sure of, as it was passed up to the Judge, jury and lawyers, who all examined it closely, and the State's Attorney said 'Mr. Lincoln, you are mistaken, the moon was just coming up instead of going down at that time' and Mr. Lincoln retorted: 'It serves my purpose just as well, just coming up, or just going down, as you admit it was not over head as Mr. Allen swore it was.' As to the question of the validity of the almanac, Mr. Lincoln's long and honorable life is a distinct refutation of any such dishonorable action on his part. My recollection of Mr. Lincoln's appearance as he addressed the jury is very vivid. The day was warm and sultry, and, as he rose to make his closing argument he removed his coat, vest, and later, his 'stock,' the old fashioned necktie worn by men in those days. His suspenders were home-made knitted ones, and finally, as he warmed up to his subject, one of them slipped from his shoulder, and he let it fall to his side, where it remained until he had finished speaking. In this 'backwoodsy' appearance he was about as homely, and awkward appearing person as could be imagined; but all this was forgotten in listening to his fiery eloquence, his masterly argument, his tender and pathetic pleading for the life of the son of his old benefactor. Tears were plentifully shed by every one present; the mother of Duff Armstrong, who was present, wore a huge sun-bonnet, her face was scarcely visible, but her feelings were plainly shown by her sobs.

As we were leaving the court room to pass into the jury room, I heard Mr. Lincoln tell Mrs. Armstrong that her boy would be cleared before sundown, which proved to be true. We were out less than an hour; only one ballot was taken, and that was unanimous for acquittal. After we rendered our verdict, Mr. Lincoln shook hands with Duff Armstrong and then led him to his mother and gave him a short lecture on making a man of himself and being a comfort to his mother, telling him to care for her and try to make as good a man as his father had been.''

Hon. J. Henry Shaw, an eminent lawyer, who practiced his profession in Cass county for many years, in writing an account of this trial said:

"He told the jury, of his once being a poor, friendless boy; that Armstrong's parents took him into their house, fed and clothed him, and gave him a home. There were tears in his eyes when he spoke. The sight of his tall, quivering frame, and the particulars of the story he so pathetically told, moved the jury to tears also, and they forgot the guilt of the defendant, in their admiration of

---

*Only two instructions were given to the jury in behalf of the defendant, and these are in the handwriting of Mr. Lincoln. A fac similie of them appears in this paper.

Fac-simile of the instructions to the Jury in behalf of the defendant. Armstrong trial, Beardstown Ill., May 7, 1858.
In Mr. Lincoln's handwriting.

his advocate. It was the most touching scene I ever witnessed."

The actual facts relative to the killing of Metzker are doubtless disclosed by these recitals in the letters to me of Mr. Brady, which are as follows:

"One of the witnesses in the Duff Armstrong case was Will Watkins, whose father lived near Petersburg, in Menard county. About two months after the Armstrong trial, T. B. Collins and myself were in the Watkins neighborhood buying cattle; Mr. Watkins sent his son Will with us, to help look up cattle. I recognized him as being the witness that Mr. Lincoln used to prove that Duff Armstrong did not have the sling-shot which was exhibited at the trial, in his possession. It naturally followed that we talked of the trial. Will Watkins told me that Mr. Lincoln sent for him to come to Springfield; he questioned him about the sling shot, and asked how it happened to be lost, and then found near the spot where Metzker was killed. He said he told Mr. Lincoln that when he laid down that night under the wagon to go to sleep, that he laid the sling shot upon the reach of the wagon, and in the morning, forgot to get it, and when the wagon was driven away, it dropped off at the place where it was found. Watkins said that he told Mr. Lincoln that he (Lincoln) did not want to use him (Watkins) as a witness, as he knew too much, and he began to tell Lincoln what he knew, and Mr. Lincoln would not allow him to tell him anything and said to Watkins: 'All I want to know is this: Did you make that slingshot? and did Duff Armstrong ever have it in his posesion?' Watkins said he replied: 'On cross-examination they may make me tell things I do not want to tell' and Mr. Lincoln assured him he would see to it that he was not questioned about anything but the slung-shot. Watkins told me that Duff Armstrong killed Metzker by striking him in the eye with an old fashioned wagon hammer and that he saw him do it. Watkins said that Douglass and all the other eight or ten witnesses for

Armstrong who swore that Armstrong hit Metzker with his fist, all swore to a lie and they knew it, as they all knew he hit him with a wagon hammer. During the trial Allen testified that Duff Armstrong hit Metzker with a sling-shot and I felt he was telling the truth until Mr. Lincoln proved by the almanac that Allen was so badly mistaken about it being a bright moonlight night; then Allen's whole testimony was discredited.''

To arrive at a sensible conclusion in this matter, I will re-capitulate the facts:

Metzker was engaged in a personal conflict, with at least two opponents, about ten o'clock of the night of August 29th, he died on the third day thereafter. A. P. Armstrong, then 17 years of age, who was present at the scene of the encounter, and who attended the trial says that at the time Metzker dragged his brother Duff off the bench or table, he spit in his face; that Duff was under the influence of whiskey; that Metzker was a large and powerful man, and Duff was one of twins, weighed about 140 pounds and not nearly so strong as Metzker; as Armstrong was so much the weaker man he would be very likely to sieze any suitable weapon, as there were numerous wagons near at hand, he doubtless grasped a wagon-hammer; that Allen in describing the encounter in court, illustrated the manner in which Duff delivered his blows, which A. P. Armstrong in my interview with him repeated to me, by raising his right hand as high as his face and striking an ''over-hand'' blow. Allen was not hostile to the Armstrong people, as he agreed with them to stay away from the trial; I have examined the records, and find that the State's Att'y caused an attachment to issue for him on May 6th, which was returned served into open court on the next day. Mr. Brady states that Allen impressed him, and the other members of the jury, as a truthful witness. Had he not made the mistake of his location of the position of the moon, it is altogether likely that the eloquence of Abraham Lincoln could not have saved his client from punishment. The files in the case

The City Hall of Beardstown, Ill., formerly the Court House of Cass County, in which Duff Armstrong was tried for murder on May 7, 1858.

show, that 15 witnesses appeared in behalf of the defendant, and it is very likely that "eight or ten" of them testified, as Will Watkins related to Mr. Brady a few weeks after the trial. A cousin of Will Watkins who lives in my city, tells me that he died several years since at his home in Menard county.

Hannah Armstrong married Samuel Wilcox, and moved to Iowa, where she died August 15, 1890, at the age of 79 years.

Duff, and three of his brothers enlisted in the civil war; about 1862, Duff was sick in an army hospital in the east; his mother wrote the President, telling him of the serious illness of her son, and asking him to send him home; Mr. Lincoln immediately sent an order for his discharge, and Duff returned to his mother, who nursed him back to health. He lived an honorable and useful life, and died in this county, on the 5th day of May, 1899, at the age of sixty-six years.

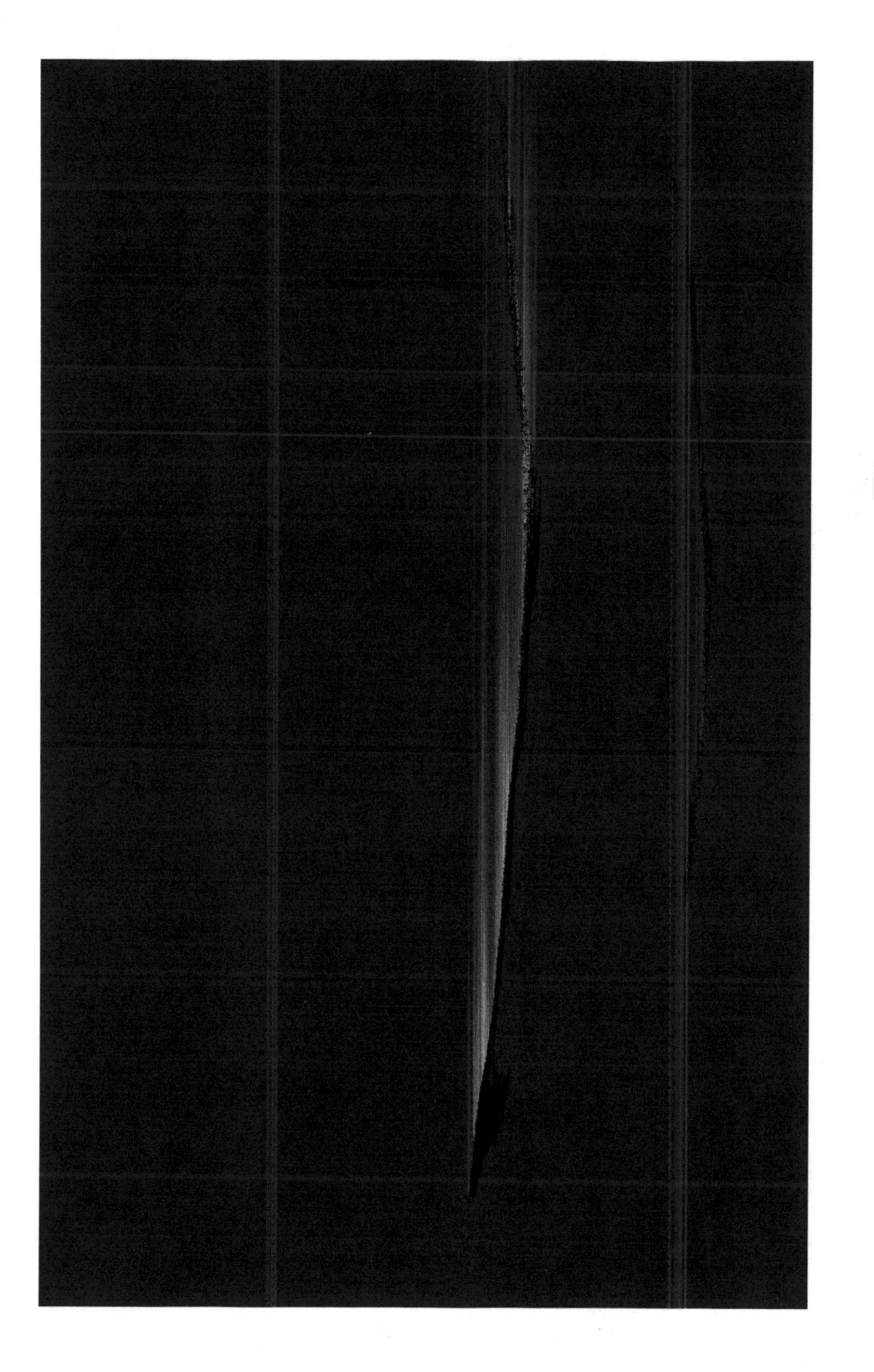